50 Japanese Street Eats Recipes

By: Kelly Johnson

Table of Contents

- Takoyaki (Octopus Balls)
- Okonomiyaki (Savory Pancake)
- Yakitori (Grilled Chicken Skewers)
- Yaki Imo (Grilled Sweet Potatoes)
- Korokke (Croquettes)
- Gyoza (Japanese Dumplings)
- Ikayaki (Grilled Squid)
- Taiyaki (Fish-Shaped Cake)
- Yakisoba (Fried Noodles)
- Onigiri (Rice Balls)
- Dango (Rice Dumplings)
- Katsu Sando (Pork Cutlet Sandwich)
- Negiyaki (Green Onion Pancake)
- Kakigori (Shaved Ice)
- Oden (Simmered Stew)
- Hōtō (Thick Noodle Soup)
- Kushi Katsu (Deep-Fried Skewers)
- Ebi Fry (Shrimp Fry)
- Nikuman (Steamed Pork Buns)
- Chikuwa (Fish Cake Skewers)
- Yaki Tori (Grilled Tofu)
- Kamaboko (Fish Cake)
- Bebi Katsu (Baby Cutlet)
- Korokke Burger (Croquette Burger)
- Soba Noodle Salad
- Shioyaki (Salt-Grilled Fish)
- Nasu Dengaku (Miso-Glazed Eggplant)
- Goya Champuru (Bitter Melon Stir-Fry)
- Tofu Burger
- Katsu Curry (Pork Cutlet Curry)
- Ramen Burger
- Satsuma Age (Fried Fish Cakes)
- Jaga Bata (Butter on Baked Potato)
- Senbei (Rice Crackers)
- Butaman (Pork Buns)
- Zaru Soba (Chilled Soba Noodles)

- Yaki Niku (Grilled Meat)
- Dorayaki (Red Bean Pancakes)
- Kani Douraku (Crab on a Stick)
- Yakimochi (Grilled Rice Cakes)
- Yaki Soba Pan (Fried Noodle Sandwich)
- Ramen (Noodle Soup)
- Baked Sweet Potato Mochi
- Katsu Don (Pork Cutlet Rice Bowl)
- Yaki Tofu (Grilled Tofu)
- Chashu (Braised Pork Belly)
- Soba Chahan (Soba Fried Rice)
- Hiyashi Chuka (Cold Chinese Noodles)
- Nikujaga (Meat and Potato Stew)
- Takosen (Takoyaki in a Senbei)

Takoyaki (Octopus Balls)

Ingredients:

- 1 cup all-purpose flour
- 1 ½ cups dashi broth
- 2 large eggs
- ½ cup cooked octopus, diced
- ¼ cup green onions, chopped
- ¼ cup pickled ginger, chopped
- Takoyaki sauce (for drizzling)
- Bonito flakes (optional, for garnish)
- Aonori (seaweed flakes, optional, for garnish)

Instructions:

1. **Make the batter**: In a bowl, whisk together flour, dashi broth, and eggs until smooth.
2. **Preheat the pan**: Heat a takoyaki pan over medium heat and lightly oil each mold.
3. **Pour the batter**: Fill each mold with batter until just full.
4. **Add filling**: Place diced octopus, green onions, and pickled ginger into each mold.
5. **Cook**: Allow the batter to cook for about 3-4 minutes, then use a skewer to turn the balls over to cook the other side until golden brown.
6. **Serve**: Drizzle with takoyaki sauce and sprinkle with bonito flakes and aonori before serving.

Okonomiyaki (Savory Pancake)

Ingredients:

- 1 cup all-purpose flour
- 1 cup dashi broth
- 2 large eggs
- 2 cups cabbage, shredded
- ½ cup green onions, chopped
- ¼ cup cooked pork belly or shrimp (optional)
- Okonomiyaki sauce (for drizzling)
- Mayonnaise (for drizzling)
- Aonori and bonito flakes (for garnish)

Instructions:

1. **Prepare the batter**: In a large bowl, mix flour and dashi broth until smooth.
2. **Add vegetables**: Stir in eggs, cabbage, green onions, and pork belly or shrimp if using.
3. **Cook**: Heat a non-stick skillet over medium heat and pour in a ladleful of batter, spreading it into a circle. Cook for about 3-4 minutes on each side until golden brown.
4. **Serve**: Drizzle with okonomiyaki sauce and mayonnaise, then sprinkle with aonori and bonito flakes.

Yakitori (Grilled Chicken Skewers)

Ingredients:

- 1 lb chicken thighs, cut into bite-sized pieces
- ½ cup soy sauce
- ¼ cup mirin
- 2 tablespoons sake
- 2 tablespoons sugar
- Green onions, cut into 1-inch pieces
- Bamboo skewers, soaked in water

Instructions:

1. **Make the marinade**: In a small saucepan, combine soy sauce, mirin, sake, and sugar. Bring to a simmer until sugar dissolves.
2. **Marinate chicken**: In a bowl, toss chicken pieces with half of the marinade and let sit for 30 minutes.
3. **Skewer chicken**: Thread chicken and green onion pieces onto bamboo skewers.
4. **Grill**: Preheat a grill or grill pan over medium heat. Cook skewers for about 10-12 minutes, brushing with remaining marinade and turning occasionally until cooked through.

Yaki Imo (Grilled Sweet Potatoes)

Ingredients:

- 2 medium sweet potatoes
- Salt (optional)

Instructions:

1. **Preheat the grill**: Preheat your grill or an oven to 400°F (200°C).
2. **Prepare sweet potatoes**: Wash the sweet potatoes and prick them with a fork.
3. **Grill**: Wrap each sweet potato in aluminum foil and place them on the grill or in the oven. Cook for 45-60 minutes, until tender.
4. **Serve**: Unwrap and enjoy hot, optionally sprinkled with a bit of salt.

Korokke (Croquettes)

Ingredients:

- 2 cups mashed potatoes
- ½ cup ground meat (beef, pork, or chicken)
- 1 onion, finely chopped
- 1 cup panko breadcrumbs
- 1 large egg, beaten
- Salt and pepper to taste
- Oil for frying

Instructions:

1. **Prepare filling**: In a skillet, cook onion until translucent. Add ground meat and cook until browned. Mix with mashed potatoes, and season with salt and pepper.
2. **Shape croquettes**: Form mixture into small patties.
3. **Coat**: Dip each patty in beaten egg, then coat with panko breadcrumbs.
4. **Fry**: Heat oil in a pan over medium heat and fry croquettes until golden brown on both sides. Drain on paper towels before serving.

Gyoza (Japanese Dumplings)

Ingredients:

- **Dough:**
    - 2 cups all-purpose flour
    - ¾ cup boiling water
- **Filling:**
    - 1 lb ground pork
    - 1 cup napa cabbage, finely chopped
    - 2 green onions, chopped
    - 1 tablespoon soy sauce
    - 1 teaspoon sesame oil
    - 1 teaspoon ginger, minced
    - 1 teaspoon garlic, minced

Instructions:

1. **Make dough**: In a bowl, mix flour and boiling water until a dough forms. Knead until smooth, then cover and let rest for 30 minutes.
2. **Prepare filling**: In a bowl, combine ground pork, cabbage, green onions, soy sauce, sesame oil, ginger, and garlic.
3. **Assemble gyoza**: Roll dough into small circles. Place a spoonful of filling in the center, then fold and pinch to seal.
4. **Cook**: Heat a non-stick skillet with oil over medium heat. Place gyoza in the skillet, add a splash of water, and cover to steam for about 5-7 minutes until cooked through and crispy on the bottom.

Ikayaki (Grilled Squid)

Ingredients:

- 1 whole squid, cleaned
- ¼ cup soy sauce
- 2 tablespoons mirin
- 1 tablespoon sake
- 1 tablespoon sugar
- Lemon wedges (for serving)

Instructions:

1. **Prepare marinade**: In a bowl, mix soy sauce, mirin, sake, and sugar.
2. **Marinate squid**: Place the cleaned squid in the marinade for 30 minutes.
3. **Grill**: Preheat the grill to medium-high heat. Grill the squid for about 3-4 minutes on each side until cooked through.
4. **Serve**: Slice the squid and serve with lemon wedges.

Taiyaki (Fish-Shaped Cake)

Ingredients:

- **Batter:**
    - 2 cups all-purpose flour
    - 1 cup milk
    - 1 large egg
    - ½ cup sugar
    - 1 tablespoon baking powder
- **Filling:**
    - 1 cup red bean paste or custard

Instructions:

1. **Make batter**: In a bowl, mix flour, milk, egg, sugar, and baking powder until smooth.
2. **Preheat mold**: Heat a taiyaki mold over medium heat and lightly grease it.
3. **Assemble**: Pour a small amount of batter into the mold, add filling, then cover with more batter.
4. **Cook**: Close the mold and cook for about 3-4 minutes on each side until golden brown.
5. **Serve**: Remove from mold and enjoy warm.

Yakisoba (Fried Noodles)

Ingredients:

- 2 servings yakisoba noodles (or any stir-fried noodles)
- 1 cup cabbage, shredded
- 1 carrot, julienned
- ½ onion, sliced
- 1 bell pepper, sliced
- ½ cup cooked protein (pork, chicken, or tofu)
- 3 tablespoons yakisoba sauce (or Worcestershire sauce)
- 2 tablespoons oil
- Pickled ginger and aonori for garnish

Instructions:

1. **Prepare the noodles**: If using fresh noodles, rinse under warm water to loosen. If using dried, cook according to package instructions.
2. **Heat oil**: In a large skillet or wok, heat oil over medium-high heat.
3. **Stir-fry vegetables**: Add onion, carrot, and bell pepper. Stir-fry for about 3-4 minutes, then add cabbage and protein, cooking until tender.
4. **Add noodles and sauce**: Add the noodles and yakisoba sauce. Toss everything together and cook for an additional 2-3 minutes.
5. **Serve**: Garnish with pickled ginger and aonori before serving.

Onigiri (Rice Balls)

Ingredients:

- 2 cups cooked sushi rice
- 1 tablespoon rice vinegar
- ½ teaspoon salt
- Fillings (tuna mayo, pickled plum, or any desired filling)
- Nori (seaweed) strips for wrapping

Instructions:

1. **Season rice**: In a bowl, mix cooked rice with rice vinegar and salt while it's still warm.
2. **Shape rice balls**: Wet your hands and take a small amount of rice, flatten it slightly, and place a teaspoon of filling in the center. Shape the rice around the filling to form a triangle or ball.
3. **Wrap**: If desired, wrap with a strip of nori.
4. **Serve**: Enjoy as a snack or lunch option.

Dango (Rice Dumplings)

Ingredients:

- 1 cup sweet rice flour (mochi flour)
- ½ cup water
- 3 tablespoons sugar
- Soy sauce (for dipping, optional)
- Sweet soy glaze (optional)

Instructions:

1. **Make dough**: In a bowl, mix sweet rice flour, water, and sugar until a smooth dough forms.
2. **Shape dumplings**: Divide the dough into small pieces and roll each into a ball.
3. **Boil**: Bring a pot of water to a boil and cook the dumplings until they float, about 3-5 minutes.
4. **Skewer and serve**: Remove and let cool slightly, then skewer onto sticks. Drizzle with sweet soy glaze or serve with soy sauce for dipping.

Katsu Sando (Pork Cutlet Sandwich)

Ingredients:

- 1 pork loin cutlet, breaded and fried
- 2 slices of shokupan (Japanese milk bread)
- Tonkatsu sauce
- Cabbage, finely shredded
- Mayonnaise (optional)

Instructions:

1. **Prepare cutlet**: Bread and fry the pork cutlet until golden and cooked through.
2. **Assemble sandwich**: Spread tonkatsu sauce on one slice of bread, add the cutlet, top with shredded cabbage, and drizzle with mayonnaise if desired.
3. **Complete sandwich**: Place the other slice of bread on top, slice in half, and serve.

Negiyaki (Green Onion Pancake)

Ingredients:

- 1 cup all-purpose flour
- 1 cup water
- ½ cup green onions, finely chopped
- 1 egg (optional)
- Salt to taste
- Oil for frying

Instructions:

1. **Make batter**: In a bowl, mix flour, water, salt, and egg until smooth.
2. **Add green onions**: Stir in chopped green onions.
3. **Cook pancakes**: Heat oil in a skillet over medium heat. Pour in a ladleful of batter, spreading it out. Cook until golden brown on one side, then flip and cook until done.
4. **Serve**: Cut into wedges and serve hot with soy sauce or dipping sauce.

Kakigori (Shaved Ice)

Ingredients:

- Ice (for shaving)
- Syrup (sweetened condensed milk, fruit syrup, or matcha syrup)
- Toppings (red beans, mochi, fruit, etc.)

Instructions:

1. **Shave ice**: Use a shaved ice machine to create fluffy ice or use a block of ice and a grater.
2. **Serve ice**: Place the shaved ice into a bowl or cup.
3. **Add syrup**: Drizzle with your choice of syrup and top with desired toppings.
4. **Enjoy**: Serve immediately and enjoy on a hot day!

Oden (Simmered Stew)

Ingredients:

- 4 cups dashi broth
- 1 daikon radish, sliced
- 4 eggs, boiled and peeled
- 1 block of tofu, cubed
- ½ cup konnyaku (konjac), sliced
- Oden ingredients (fish cakes, mushrooms, etc.)
- Soy sauce and mirin (for seasoning)

Instructions:

1. **Prepare broth**: In a pot, heat dashi broth, soy sauce, and mirin.
2. **Add ingredients**: Add daikon, boiled eggs, tofu, konnyaku, and any additional oden ingredients.
3. **Simmer**: Cook over low heat for about 30-40 minutes until flavors meld and daikon is tender.
4. **Serve**: Serve hot in bowls with broth and enjoy as a comforting dish.

Hōtō (Thick Noodle Soup)

Ingredients:

- 2 cups thick udon noodles (or homemade hōtō noodles)
- 4 cups dashi or chicken broth
- 1 cup seasonal vegetables (pumpkin, mushrooms, leafy greens)
- 1 tablespoon soy sauce
- 1 tablespoon miso (optional)
- Green onions for garnish

Instructions:

1. **Prepare broth**: In a pot, bring the broth to a boil and add soy sauce and miso if using.
2. **Add vegetables**: Add seasonal vegetables and cook until tender.
3. **Cook noodles**: Add thick noodles and simmer until noodles are cooked through.
4. **Serve**: Garnish with chopped green onions before serving hot.

Kushi Katsu (Deep-Fried Skewers)

Ingredients:

- 1 pound pork loin, cut into bite-sized pieces
- 1 cup panko breadcrumbs
- ½ cup all-purpose flour
- 2 eggs, beaten
- Skewers
- Oil for frying
- Tonkatsu sauce for serving

Instructions:

1. **Prepare skewers**: Thread pieces of pork onto skewers.
2. **Coat skewers**: Dredge each skewer in flour, dip in beaten eggs, then coat with panko breadcrumbs.
3. **Heat oil**: In a deep pan, heat oil to 350°F (175°C).
4. **Fry skewers**: Fry skewers until golden brown and cooked through, about 3-4 minutes.
5. **Serve**: Drain on paper towels and serve with tonkatsu sauce.

Ebi Fry (Shrimp Fry)

Ingredients:

- 1 pound large shrimp, peeled and deveined
- 1 cup panko breadcrumbs
- ½ cup all-purpose flour
- 2 eggs, beaten
- Oil for frying
- Tonkatsu sauce or tartar sauce for serving

Instructions:

1. **Prepare shrimp**: Dredge shrimp in flour, dip in beaten eggs, then coat with panko breadcrumbs.
2. **Heat oil**: In a deep pan, heat oil to 350°F (175°C).
3. **Fry shrimp**: Fry shrimp until golden brown and cooked through, about 2-3 minutes.
4. **Serve**: Drain on paper towels and serve with tonkatsu sauce or tartar sauce.

Nikuman (Steamed Pork Buns)

Ingredients:

- 2 cups all-purpose flour
- 2 tablespoons sugar
- 1 teaspoon instant yeast
- ¾ cup warm water
- 1 pound ground pork
- 2 green onions, chopped
- 1 tablespoon soy sauce
- 1 teaspoon sesame oil
- Salt and pepper to taste

Instructions:

1. **Make dough**: In a bowl, combine flour, sugar, yeast, and warm water. Knead until smooth. Let rise for 1 hour.
2. **Prepare filling**: In another bowl, mix ground pork, green onions, soy sauce, sesame oil, salt, and pepper.
3. **Shape buns**: Divide dough into small balls, flatten each, place a spoonful of filling in the center, and pinch to seal.
4. **Steam buns**: Place buns in a steamer and steam for 15-20 minutes until cooked.
5. **Serve**: Enjoy warm.

Chikuwa (Fish Cake Skewers)

Ingredients:

- 1 cup fish paste (surimi)
- 1 tablespoon starch (potato or cornstarch)
- 1 tablespoon soy sauce
- Skewers
- Oil for frying

Instructions:

1. **Make fish cakes**: In a bowl, mix fish paste, starch, and soy sauce until smooth.
2. **Shape and skewer**: Mold the mixture around skewers to form a tube shape.
3. **Heat oil**: In a pan, heat oil over medium heat.
4. **Fry skewers**: Fry skewers until golden and cooked through, about 5-7 minutes.
5. **Serve**: Enjoy hot, optionally with soy sauce for dipping.

Yaki Tori (Grilled Tofu)

Ingredients:

- 1 block firm tofu, pressed and cut into cubes
- 2 tablespoons soy sauce
- 1 tablespoon mirin
- 1 tablespoon sesame oil
- Skewers
- Green onions for garnish

Instructions:

1. **Marinate tofu**: In a bowl, mix soy sauce, mirin, and sesame oil. Add tofu cubes and marinate for 30 minutes.
2. **Skewer tofu**: Thread marinated tofu onto skewers.
3. **Grill tofu**: Preheat a grill or grill pan over medium heat. Grill skewers until golden brown, about 3-4 minutes per side.
4. **Serve**: Garnish with green onions before serving.

Kamaboko (Fish Cake)

Ingredients:

- 1 pound fish paste (surimi)
- 1 tablespoon sugar
- 1 tablespoon salt
- 1 tablespoon starch (potato or cornstarch)
- Nori (seaweed) for wrapping

Instructions:

1. **Make mixture**: In a bowl, combine fish paste, sugar, salt, and starch. Mix until smooth.
2. **Shape fish cake**: Mold the mixture into a log shape.
3. **Wrap with nori**: Wrap the log with nori if desired.
4. **Steam fish cake**: Steam for 30 minutes until cooked through.
5. **Serve**: Slice and serve as a side dish or snack.

Bebi Katsu (Baby Cutlet)

Ingredients:

- 1 pound ground meat (chicken, pork, or beef)
- 1 egg, beaten
- 1 cup panko breadcrumbs
- ½ cup all-purpose flour
- Oil for frying

Instructions:

1. **Shape cutlets**: Form small patties from the ground meat mixture.
2. **Coat cutlets**: Dredge each patty in flour, dip in beaten egg, and coat with panko breadcrumbs.
3. **Heat oil**: In a deep pan, heat oil to 350°F (175°C).
4. **Fry cutlets**: Fry until golden brown and cooked through, about 4-5 minutes.
5. **Serve**: Drain on paper towels and serve with dipping sauce.

Korokke Burger (Croquette Burger)

Ingredients:

- 2 large potatoes, boiled and mashed
- 1 cup ground meat (beef or chicken)
- 1 onion, finely chopped
- 1 egg, beaten
- 1 cup panko breadcrumbs
- 4 burger buns
- Lettuce and tomato for toppings
- Oil for frying

Instructions:

1. **Prepare filling**: In a pan, sauté onion until soft. Add ground meat and cook until browned. Mix with mashed potatoes.
2. **Shape patties**: Form the mixture into patties.
3. **Coat patties**: Dip each patty in beaten egg and coat with panko breadcrumbs.
4. **Fry patties**: Heat oil in a pan and fry patties until golden brown on both sides.
5. **Assemble burgers**: Place patties on burger buns with lettuce and tomato. Serve warm.

Soba Noodle Salad

Ingredients:

- 8 ounces soba noodles
- 1 cup cucumber, julienned
- 1 cup carrots, julienned
- ½ cup green onions, sliced
- ¼ cup soy sauce
- 2 tablespoons sesame oil
- 1 tablespoon rice vinegar
- 1 tablespoon sesame seeds

Instructions:

1. **Cook noodles**: Boil soba noodles according to package instructions. Drain and rinse under cold water.
2. **Prepare dressing**: In a bowl, whisk together soy sauce, sesame oil, and rice vinegar.
3. **Combine ingredients**: In a large bowl, combine cooled noodles, cucumber, carrots, and green onions.
4. **Add dressing**: Pour dressing over the salad and toss to combine.
5. **Serve**: Garnish with sesame seeds and serve chilled.

Shioyaki (Salt-Grilled Fish)

Ingredients:

- 2 whole fish (such as mackerel or sea bream), cleaned
- 2 tablespoons salt
- Lemon wedges for serving

Instructions:

1. **Salt fish**: Rub salt all over the fish, including the cavity. Let it sit for 30 minutes.
2. **Preheat grill**: Heat the grill to medium-high.
3. **Grill fish**: Place fish on the grill and cook for about 5-7 minutes on each side until cooked through and skin is crispy.
4. **Serve**: Serve with lemon wedges.

Nasu Dengaku (Miso-Glazed Eggplant)

Ingredients:

- 2 medium eggplants, halved
- ¼ cup miso paste
- 2 tablespoons sugar
- 2 tablespoons mirin
- 1 tablespoon soy sauce
- Green onions for garnish

Instructions:

1. **Preheat oven**: Preheat the oven to 400°F (200°C).
2. **Prepare eggplant**: Score the flesh of the eggplant halves and place them cut-side up on a baking sheet.
3. **Make miso glaze**: In a bowl, mix miso paste, sugar, mirin, and soy sauce until smooth.
4. **Glaze eggplant**: Spread the miso mixture over the cut sides of the eggplants.
5. **Bake**: Bake for 20-25 minutes until eggplants are tender and miso is caramelized. Garnish with green onions before serving.

Goya Champuru (Bitter Melon Stir-Fry)

Ingredients:

- 1 large bitter melon, sliced
- 1 cup tofu, cubed
- 1 cup pork or chicken, sliced (optional)
- 2 tablespoons soy sauce
- 1 tablespoon sesame oil
- 2 cloves garlic, minced
- 2 green onions, sliced

Instructions:

1. **Prepare tofu**: In a pan, heat sesame oil and fry the tofu until golden. Remove and set aside.
2. **Stir-fry meat**: In the same pan, stir-fry pork or chicken until cooked through.
3. **Add bitter melon**: Add bitter melon and garlic, cooking until the melon is tender.
4. **Combine**: Add the tofu back to the pan and pour in soy sauce. Stir well.
5. **Serve**: Garnish with green onions and serve hot.

Tofu Burger

Ingredients:

- 1 block firm tofu, pressed and crumbled
- 1 cup breadcrumbs
- 1/4 cup green onions, chopped
- 2 tablespoons soy sauce
- 1 tablespoon sesame oil
- 1 teaspoon garlic powder
- Burger buns and toppings of choice

Instructions:

1. **Mix ingredients**: In a bowl, combine crumbled tofu, breadcrumbs, green onions, soy sauce, sesame oil, and garlic powder. Mix well.
2. **Shape patties**: Form the mixture into burger patties.
3. **Cook patties**: In a skillet, heat oil over medium heat and cook patties until golden brown on both sides, about 4-5 minutes per side.
4. **Assemble burgers**: Serve on buns with your favorite toppings.

Katsu Curry (Pork Cutlet Curry)

Ingredients:

- 2 pork loin cutlets
- Salt and pepper to taste
- 1 cup panko breadcrumbs
- 1 egg, beaten
- ½ cup flour
- 2 cups curry sauce (store-bought or homemade)
- Cooked rice for serving

Instructions:

1. **Prepare pork**: Season pork cutlets with salt and pepper. Dredge in flour, dip in egg, and coat with panko breadcrumbs.
2. **Fry cutlets**: Heat oil in a pan and fry the cutlets until golden brown and cooked through, about 4-5 minutes per side.
3. **Heat curry**: In a saucepan, heat the curry sauce until warmed through.
4. **Serve**: Slice the cutlets and serve over rice, topped with curry sauce.

Ramen Burger

Ingredients:

- 2 cups cooked ramen noodles
- 1 egg, beaten
- ½ cup cooked ground beef or pork
- Soy sauce to taste
- Burger toppings of choice (lettuce, tomato, etc.)

Instructions:

1. **Prepare noodles**: In a bowl, mix cooked ramen noodles with the beaten egg.
2. **Form patties**: Shape the noodle mixture into burger patties.
3. **Cook patties**: In a skillet, fry noodle patties until crispy on both sides, about 3-4 minutes.
4. **Assemble burgers**: Top each ramen patty with cooked ground meat and your favorite burger toppings.

Satsuma Age (Fried Fish Cakes)

Ingredients:

- 1 pound fish paste (surimi)
- ½ cup chopped vegetables (carrots, green onions)
- 1 tablespoon soy sauce
- Oil for frying

Instructions:

1. **Mix ingredients**: In a bowl, combine fish paste, chopped vegetables, and soy sauce.
2. **Shape cakes**: Form small cakes from the mixture.
3. **Heat oil**: In a pan, heat oil over medium heat.
4. **Fry cakes**: Fry the fish cakes until golden brown and cooked through, about 4-5 minutes.
5. **Serve**: Drain on paper towels and serve hot.

Jaga Bata (Butter on Baked Potato)

Ingredients:

- 4 medium-sized potatoes
- 4 tablespoons butter
- Salt to taste

Instructions:

1. **Preheat oven**: Preheat the oven to 400°F (200°C).
2. **Bake potatoes**: Wash and prick the potatoes with a fork. Bake them directly on the oven rack for about 45-60 minutes until tender.
3. **Serve**: Cut open the potatoes, add butter, and sprinkle with salt before serving.

Senbei (Rice Crackers)

Ingredients:

- 2 cups glutinous rice flour
- ½ cup water
- 2 tablespoons soy sauce
- Sesame seeds for topping

Instructions:

1. **Make dough**: In a bowl, combine glutinous rice flour, water, and soy sauce. Mix until it forms a dough.
2. **Shape crackers**: Divide the dough into small balls and flatten them into thin discs.
3. **Bake**: Preheat the oven to 350°F (175°C). Place the discs on a baking sheet and bake for about 15-20 minutes until crispy.
4. **Cool**: Let the crackers cool and sprinkle with sesame seeds before serving.

Butaman (Pork Buns)

Ingredients:

- 2 cups all-purpose flour
- 1 tablespoon sugar
- 1 teaspoon baking powder
- ½ cup warm water
- 1 tablespoon yeast
- 1 cup ground pork
- 2 tablespoons soy sauce
- 1 tablespoon ginger, grated

Instructions:

1. **Make dough**: In a bowl, combine flour, sugar, baking powder, and yeast. Add warm water and knead until smooth. Let rise for 1 hour.
2. **Prepare filling**: In another bowl, mix ground pork, soy sauce, and ginger.
3. **Shape buns**: Divide the dough into small pieces, flatten them, and place a spoonful of filling in the center. Pinch to seal.
4. **Steam buns**: Steam the buns for about 15-20 minutes until cooked through.

Zaru Soba (Chilled Soba Noodles)

Ingredients:

- 8 ounces soba noodles
- ¼ cup soy sauce
- 2 tablespoons mirin
- 1 tablespoon wasabi (optional)
- Green onions and nori for garnish

Instructions:

1. **Cook soba**: Boil the soba noodles according to package instructions. Drain and rinse under cold water.
2. **Prepare dipping sauce**: In a bowl, mix soy sauce and mirin.
3. **Serve**: Serve the chilled noodles with dipping sauce, garnished with green onions and nori.

Yaki Niku (Grilled Meat)

Ingredients:

- 1 pound beef or pork, thinly sliced
- 2 tablespoons soy sauce
- 1 tablespoon mirin
- 1 tablespoon sesame oil
- 1 tablespoon garlic, minced

Instructions:

1. **Marinate meat**: In a bowl, combine soy sauce, mirin, sesame oil, and garlic. Add meat and marinate for at least 30 minutes.
2. **Grill meat**: Preheat a grill or skillet. Grill the marinated meat until cooked through, about 3-4 minutes per side.
3. **Serve**: Serve with rice and vegetables.

Dorayaki (Red Bean Pancakes)

Ingredients:

- 1 cup all-purpose flour
- 2 eggs
- ½ cup sugar
- 1 teaspoon baking powder
- ½ cup red bean paste

Instructions:

1. **Make batter**: In a bowl, mix flour, eggs, sugar, and baking powder until smooth.
2. **Cook pancakes**: Heat a non-stick skillet over medium heat. Pour a small amount of batter to form a pancake. Cook until bubbles form, then flip and cook until golden brown.
3. **Assemble**: Place a spoonful of red bean paste between two pancakes to form a sandwich.

Kani Douraku (Crab on a Stick)

Ingredients:

- 1 pound crab meat (or imitation crab)
- 2 tablespoons soy sauce
- 1 tablespoon lemon juice
- Skewers

Instructions:

1. **Prepare crab**: In a bowl, combine crab meat with soy sauce and lemon juice.
2. **Skewer crab**: Thread the crab mixture onto skewers.
3. **Grill**: Grill over medium heat for about 5-7 minutes until heated through.

Yakimochi (Grilled Rice Cakes)

Ingredients:

- 2 cups mochiko (sweet rice flour)
- 1 cup water
- Soy sauce or sweet soy sauce for serving

Instructions:

1. **Make dough**: In a bowl, combine mochiko and water. Mix until it forms a smooth dough.
2. **Shape cakes**: Divide the dough into small pieces and shape into flat cakes.
3. **Grill**: Grill the rice cakes over medium heat until golden and crispy on both sides.
4. **Serve**: Serve with soy sauce or sweet soy sauce for dipping.

Yaki Soba Pan (Fried Noodle Sandwich)

Ingredients:

- 2 servings of yaki soba (fried noodles)
- 4 soft sandwich rolls
- 2 tablespoons mayonnaise
- Sliced green onions and pickled ginger for garnish

Instructions:

1. **Prepare yaki soba**: Cook yaki soba according to package instructions.
2. **Assemble sandwiches**: Slice the sandwich rolls open and spread mayonnaise inside.
3. **Fill rolls**: Fill each roll with a generous portion of yaki soba, garnishing with green onions and pickled ginger.
4. **Serve**: Serve warm as a unique sandwich.

Ramen (Noodle Soup)

Ingredients:

- 4 cups chicken or pork broth
- 2 servings of ramen noodles
- 2 soft-boiled eggs
- 1 cup sliced chashu (braised pork belly)
- Green onions and nori for garnish

Instructions:

1. **Heat broth**: In a pot, bring the broth to a simmer.
2. **Cook noodles**: Add ramen noodles to the broth and cook according to package instructions.
3. **Serve**: Ladle noodles and broth into bowls, topping with sliced chashu, soft-boiled eggs, green onions, and nori.

Baked Sweet Potato Mochi

Ingredients:

- 2 medium sweet potatoes
- 1 cup mochiko (sweet rice flour)
- ½ cup sugar
- Cornstarch for dusting

Instructions:

1. **Bake sweet potatoes**: Preheat the oven to 400°F (200°C). Bake sweet potatoes until tender, about 45 minutes.
2. **Make mochi dough**: Mash the sweet potatoes and combine with mochiko and sugar. Mix until a smooth dough forms.
3. **Shape mochi**: Dust hands with cornstarch and shape the dough into small balls.
4. **Serve**: Enjoy as a sweet snack or dessert.

Katsu Don (Pork Cutlet Rice Bowl)

Ingredients:

- 2 pork cutlets (tonkatsu)
- 2 cups cooked rice
- 2 eggs
- ¼ cup dashi or chicken broth
- 2 tablespoons soy sauce
- Sliced green onions for garnish

Instructions:

1. **Prepare tonkatsu**: Cook pork cutlets until golden and crispy, then slice them.
2. **Make sauce**: In a pan, combine dashi, soy sauce, and eggs. Heat gently, stirring until eggs are set.
3. **Assemble bowl**: Place cooked rice in a bowl, top with sliced tonkatsu, and pour the egg mixture over.
4. **Serve**: Garnish with green onions before serving.

Yaki Tofu (Grilled Tofu)

Ingredients:

- 1 block firm tofu
- 2 tablespoons soy sauce
- 1 tablespoon sesame oil
- Green onions for garnish

Instructions:

1. **Prepare tofu**: Press tofu to remove excess water and cut into slices.
2. **Marinate**: In a bowl, mix soy sauce and sesame oil. Marinate tofu slices for at least 30 minutes.
3. **Grill tofu**: Preheat a grill or skillet and cook tofu until golden brown on both sides.
4. **Serve**: Garnish with sliced green onions before serving.

Chashu (Braised Pork Belly)

Ingredients:

- 2 pounds pork belly
- ½ cup soy sauce
- ½ cup mirin
- ½ cup sake
- ¼ cup sugar

Instructions:

1. **Sear pork**: In a pot, sear the pork belly on all sides until browned.
2. **Braised sauce**: Add soy sauce, mirin, sake, and sugar to the pot. Bring to a simmer.
3. **Braised pork**: Cover and simmer for 2-3 hours until tender, flipping occasionally.
4. **Slice and serve**: Slice the pork and serve it with ramen or rice.

Soba Chahan (Soba Fried Rice)

Ingredients:

- 2 servings of cooked soba noodles
- 1 cup mixed vegetables (carrots, peas, corn)
- 2 eggs
- 2 tablespoons soy sauce
- Green onions for garnish

Instructions:

1. **Stir-fry vegetables**: In a pan, stir-fry mixed vegetables until tender.
2. **Add soba**: Add cooked soba noodles to the pan and stir-fry together.
3. **Add eggs**: Push the noodles to one side and scramble the eggs on the other side. Mix everything together and add soy sauce.
4. **Serve**: Garnish with sliced green onions before serving.

Hiyashi Chuka (Cold Chinese Noodles)

Ingredients:

- 2 servings of chilled ramen noodles
- ½ cucumber, julienned
- 1 carrot, julienned
- 2 boiled eggs, halved
- ¼ cup ham, sliced
- Soy sauce and sesame oil for dressing

Instructions:

1. **Prepare ingredients**: Cook and chill ramen noodles. Prepare vegetables and toppings.
2. **Assemble**: Place chilled noodles on a plate and arrange cucumber, carrot, eggs, and ham on top.
3. **Dress**: Drizzle with soy sauce and sesame oil before serving.

Nikujaga (Meat and Potato Stew)

Ingredients:

- 1 pound beef (sliced thin)
- 3 medium potatoes (peeled and cut into chunks)
- 1 onion (sliced)
- 1 cup carrots (sliced)
- ¼ cup soy sauce
- 2 tablespoons sugar
- 2 cups dashi or beef broth
- 2 tablespoons mirin
- Green onions for garnish

Instructions:

1. **Sauté ingredients**: In a pot, sauté the beef and onion until the beef is browned.
2. **Add vegetables**: Add potatoes and carrots, stirring to combine.
3. **Add broth and seasonings**: Pour in the dashi, soy sauce, sugar, and mirin. Bring to a boil.
4. **Simmer**: Reduce heat, cover, and simmer until vegetables are tender, about 20-30 minutes.
5. **Serve**: Garnish with sliced green onions before serving.

Takosen (Takoyaki in a Senbei)

Ingredients:

- 1 batch of takoyaki batter (flour, dashi, eggs, and chopped octopus)
- 4 senbei (rice crackers)
- Takoyaki sauce
- Aonori (seaweed flakes)
- Bonito flakes for garnish

Instructions:

1. **Make takoyaki**: Prepare takoyaki using a takoyaki grill, cooking until golden brown and crispy.
2. **Assemble senbei**: Place a piece of takoyaki on each senbei.
3. **Garnish**: Drizzle takoyaki sauce over the top, sprinkle with aonori and bonito flakes.
4. **Serve**: Enjoy as a delicious snack or appetizer.

www.ingramcontent.com/pod-product-compliance
Lightning Source LLC
LaVergne TN
LVHW081340060526
838201LV00055B/2764